Overwhelmed?

Finding Help in Psalm 37

Devotional & Journal

Other Books by Bonita M. Sparks Adams Include:

ACTIVATE: Secret Agents in Spiritual Warfare

Miracles: They Happen Every Day

Exposing the Truth About the Holidays thru Drama

Exposed Bible Study Guide (An accompaniment to the stage play)

For More Information Contact:

Write The Vision Publishing LLC
Maumee, OH
Email: writethevisionpub@gmail.com

Overwhelmed?

Finding Help in Psalm 37

Devotional & Journal

By
Bonita M. Sparks Adams

Foreword by: Rev. Dr. Eric Leake

Published By

Write The Vision Publishing LLC
Maumee, OH

Copyright © 2019 by Bonita Marie (Sparks) Adams

All rights reserved. This book is protected by the copyright laws of the United States of America. No part of this book may be reproduced or transmitted in any form or by any means, electronic, mechanical, photocopying, or otherwise, without prior written consent of the publisher, except for the inclusion of brief quotations in a review.

Unless otherwise noted, all biblical passages referenced employ the New International Version.

Published by
WRITE THE VISION PUBLISHING LLC, Maumee, Ohio
Email: writethevisionpub@gmail.com

Limit of Liability/Disclaimer of Warranty: While the publisher and author have used their best efforts in preparing this book, they make no representations or warranties with respect to the accuracy or completeness of the contents of this book and specifically disclaim any implied warranties of merchantability or fitness for a particular purpose. No warranty may be created or extended by sales reps or written sales materials. The advice and strategies contained herein may not be suitable for your situation. Consult with a professional where appropriate. Neither the publisher nor author shall be liable for any loss of profit or any other commercial damages, including but not limited to special, incidental, consequential or other damages.

ISBN: 978-1-7344589-3-0

Edited by: So It Is Written LLC

Cover design by: Melissa Talbot

Model on Cover: Tamika C. Adams-Sajdak DC

Photography by: Marcus Hamilton & Jeff Summers

Printed in the United States of America

Dedication

I dedicate this book to my mother, Rev. Shirley A. Sparks, father, Ronald L. Sparks, Sr., and husband, James L. Adams. I am forever grateful and thankful for the love and support you each have given me down through the years.

Table of Contents

Foreword..ix

Acknowledgements...xi

Prayer xv

Introduction 1

Psalm 37 (New International Version).......................5

PART 1: I AM DEALING WITH...

LESSON 1: Opposition All Around 13

LESSON 2: Difficult People.. 17

LESSON 3: Feeling Insecure 21

LESSON 4: What About What I Want? 27

LESSON 5: Deadline Approaching 33

LESSON 6: Financial Problems 37

LESSON 7: Angry & Stressed Out 43

LESSON 8: Not Enough...I Need More 49

LESSON 9: Plotting & Scheming Against Me 55
LESSON 10: Stuck & Not Moving Forward 61
LESSON 11: I'm So Tired of This 67

PART 2: GOD's PROMISES TO ME

LESSON 12: "I'm Under His Care" 75
LESSON 13: "I Have Plenty" 79
LESSON 14: "My Enemies Will Be Dealt With" 83
LESSON 15: "I Have an Inheritance" 87
LESSON 16: "He's Holding Me Up" 93
LESSON 17: "He Will Not Forsake Me" 97
LESSON 18: "He Has a Place for Me" 101
LESSON 19: "He Loves Me" 105
LESSON 20: "I Am Wise" 109
LESSON 21: "He is in My Heart So I Walk Right" 113
LESSON 22: "Wicked Will Not Triumph Over Me" 117
LESSON 23: "He Will Exalt Me" 121
LESSON 24: "He Has a Good Future For Me" 125
LESSON 25: "He Saved Me" 127
About The Author 131

Foreword

For many years, Psalm 37 has been a favorite and foundational Scripture for my wife, Jean, and me. It has given us consolation and confirmation, over and over again, that God intervenes in the affairs of humans in the midst of evil and danger. In *Overwhelmed? Finding Help in Psalm 37, A Devotional and Journal*, Bonita Sparks Adams lays out a unique plan to cope with being overwhelmed.

She points out various difficulties and challenges that we face in this culture of busyness with life, family, work and ministry. Likewise, she offers us hope that the Lord, who helps us, will handle evil of every kind. If you are *overwhelmed*, prepare to be enriched, encouraged and empowered each day as you use this Holy Spirit inspired work from God's servant, Bonita Adams.

Rev. Dr. Eric Leake, Pastor
Author of *Praying on Purpose*

Acknowledgements

First, I'm thankful for my faith and the personal relationship I have with the Father, Son and Holy Spirit. These have brought comfort to me, guided my decisions, been with me and answered my many prayers when I have felt overwhelmed. Without my knowledge of you and your presence in my daily life, I would not have survived.

Secondly, I thank those who helped with the publishing of this book. Rev. Dr. Eric Leake, thank you for writing the foreword. Mom, Pastor Shirley A. Sparks, thank you for your prayer for all those reading this book. Tenita Johnson of So It Is Written, LLC, thank you for your advice and editorial services. Valerie J. Lewis Coleman, thank you for your self-publishing insight. Melissa Talbot, thank you for designing my cover and logo and, Tamika C. Adams-Sajdak DC, thank you for gracing

Overwhelmed?

the cover. Marcus Hamilton and Jeff Summers, thank you for your photography.

Last, but not least, I'm thankful for my entire earthly family. God used each one of you, in your own way, at different times in my life to help, encourage or provide me with whatever I needed at the time. Your presence in my life helped me get through those challenges. I cannot name every family member, but I want to especially acknowledge the following family members who played a special role in my life at a time when I was feeling *overwhelmed*:

Ronald L. Sparks, Sr. & Rev. Shirley A. Sparks
(Parents)

James L. Adams
(Husband)

Dr. Samantha P. Adams & Paul Adams
(Mother-in-Law/Father-in-Law, In Memory)

LaTosha (Jason), Tamika (Lukasz) & Aria
(Children & Granddaughter)

Ronald L. Sparks, Jr.
(Brother)

Dr. Karen Adams-Ferguson
(Sister-in-Law/Best Friend)

Bonita M. Sparks Adams

Cecelia, Denise & Candace
(Sisters-in-Law)

Paula Duckworth
(Sister-in-Law, In Memory)

Nate & Edward
(Brothers-in-Law)

Betty, Phyllis, Marilyn, Barbara Ann,
Helen & Charlotte
(Aunts)

Glacie Reed
(Aunt, In Memory)

Donald
(Uncle)

Harold, Wallace & Sonny
(Uncles, In Memory)

Many cousins, nieces and nephews

Prayer

Dear Heavenly Father,

I thank you for giving Bonita the revelation and obedience to write this book.

My prayer is that everyone who reads this book will come to know God as Jehovah Jireh, one who has prevision and makes provision. Experiencing Him in this way will give them the faith to cast all of their cares on Him. They will become confident that He is able to meet every one of their needs, according to His riches in glory by Christ Jesus. Then, God can use them as an ambassador so others will come to know Him as a provider.

I decree and declare this done, and I thank you. In the mighty, majestic name of Jesus, I pray. Amen.

Rev. Shirley A. Sparks, Pastor
Walls Memorial Chapel AME Zion Church of Toledo, OH

Introduction

I wear many hats! I am a mother, wife, daughter, sister, niece, cousin and aunt.

I am a Christian who serves as a preacher steward; teacher of Sunday school; teacher of Bible study and Vacation Bible School; prayer warrior; and I sing on the praise & worship team. I pray and counsel others. I extend the gift of helps, when needed, along with sharing my faith.

I am a high-school business teacher who's active in several programs at the school, including but not limited to: business department chairperson and advisor of the African-American Club; I am a facilitator for a Chick-fil-A Leadership Academy; I am on the Diversity Team, Career Pathways Committee, Extra-Curricular Pay Committee, Technology Committee and the Credit Flexibility Committee. I also tutor for my school district after school.

Overwhelmed?

I am a writer. I've written plays, books and the curriculum for educational and religious purposes.

I am an entrepreneur. With my husband, we own and operate a real estate business and our production company, where we produce plays and other programs. I also am a Mary Kay beauty consultant!

List Your Roles:

_____

_____

_____

_____

_____

All of these roles have responsibilities attached to them. People don't always cooperate. Sometimes you don't have enough help, time, money, energy or knowledge to do what's needed. No wonder why we are feeling *overwhelmed!* All of this was wearing on me, and the Lord comforted me through Psalm 37, which led me to write this devotional. *Overwhelmed? Finding Help in Psalm 37: Devotional & Journal* is designed to help you experience peace of mind, comfort, encouragement and strength, in spite of what you may be

Bonita M. Sparks Adams

going through. My prayer is that, as you read this book, God will speak to your heart regarding matters that personally concern you, enabling you to reflect and take actions that will help change your mindset and life.

Since each topic is based on specific verses found in Psalm 37, you should read the designated verses given at the top of the page prior to reading the given devotional to get the most out of it. Psalm 37 is included in its entirety at the beginning of this book. All Scriptures used/and or referred to in this book are from the New International Version of the Bible, unless noted otherwise.

You can read a lesson each day consecutively, spend several days on one lesson, or jump around. Whatever works best for you, follow that plan.

Psalm 37
(New International Version)

1. *Do not fret because of those who are evil, or be envious of those who do wrong;*
2. *for like the grass they will soon wither, like green plants they will soon die away.*
3. *Trust in the LORD, and do good; dwell in the land, and enjoy safe pasture.*
4. *Take delight in the LORD, and he will give you the desires of your heart.*
5. *Commit your way to the LORD; trust in him, and he will do this:*
6. *He will make your righteous reward shine like the dawn, your vindication like the noonday sun.*
7. *Be still before the LORD and wait patiently for him; do not fret when people succeed in*

Overwhelmed?

their ways, when they carry out their wicked schemes.

8 *Refrain from anger and turn from wrath; do not fret – it leads only to evil.*

9 *For those who are evil will be destroyed, but those who hope in the LORD will inherit the land.*

10 *A little while, and the wicked will be no more; though you look for them, they will not be found.*

11 *But the meek will inherit the land and enjoy peace and prosperity.*

12 *The wicked plot against the righteous and gnash their teeth at them;*

13 *but the Lord laughs at the wicked, for he knows their day is coming.*

14 *The wicked draw the sword and bend the bow to bring down the poor and needy, to slay those whose ways are upright.*

15 *But their swords will pierce their own hearts, and their bows will be broken.*

16 *Better the little that the righteous have than the wealth of many wicked;*

17 *for the power of the wicked will be broken, but the LORD upholds the righteous.*

18 *The blameless spend their days under the LORD's care, and their inheritance will endure forever.*

19 *In times of disaster they will not wither; in days of famine they will enjoy plenty.*

20 *But the wicked will perish: Though the LORD's enemies are like the flowers of the field, they will be consumed, they will go up in smoke.*

21 *The wicked borrow and do not repay, but the righteous give generously;*

22 *Those the LORD blesses will inherit the land, but those he curses will be destroyed.*

23 *The LORD makes firm the steps of the one who delights in him;*

24 *though he may stumble, he will not fall, for the LORD upholds him with his hand.*

25 *I was young and now I am old, yet I have never seen the righteous forsaken or their children begging bread.*

26 *They are always generous and lend freely; their children will be a blessing.*

Overwhelmed?

27 Turn from evil and do good; then you will dwell in the land forever.

28 For the LORD loves the just and will not forsake his faithful ones. Wrongdoers will be completely destroyed; the offspring of the wicked will perish.

29 The righteous will inherit the land and dwell in it forever.

30 The mouths of the righteous utter wisdom, and their tongues speak what is just.

31 The law of their God is in their hearts; their feet do not slip.

32 The wicked lie in wait for the righteous, intent on putting them to death;

33 but the LORD will not leave them in the power of the wicked or let them be condemned when brought to trial.

34 Hope in the LORD and keep his way. He will exalt you to inherit the land; when the wicked are destroyed, you will see it.

35 I have seen a wicked and ruthless man flourishing like a luxuriant native tree,

36 *but he soon passed away and was no more; though I looked for him, he could not be found.*

37 *Consider the blameless, observe the upright; a future awaits those who seek peace.*

38 *But all sinners will be destroyed; there will be no future for the wicked.*

39 *The salvation of the righteous comes from the LORD; he is their stronghold in time of trouble.*

40 *The LORD helps them and delivers them; he delivers them from the wicked and saves them, because they take refuge in him.*

PART 1:
I AM DEALING WITH...

(Read Psalm 37:1)
Lesson 1:
Opposition All Around

When you try to do good, evil will try to oppose you (Romans 7:21). Instead of feeling bad about the opposition, take it as a sign that you must be doing something right! God always sides with the one who is doing the right things! Keep doing the right things! God will fight your battles. Even though sometimes it looks like those who are doing wrong are prospering and getting ahead, it is only for a season!

During the summer, plants are green and the flowers are blooming; the days are longer and sunny. You can enjoy doing many things outside. However, it only lasts for a few months—if you live in the Midwest like I do! Winter eventually comes, and those plants and flowers die. Days get shorter and many retreat inside because they don't want

Overwhelmed?

to be outside in the cold! The "tables will turn" and a day is coming for those who are doing wrong to suffer the consequences of their actions. This is not a table you want to be sitting at. Instead, you are unknowingly already receiving blessings from the Lord for doing what is right. Other blessings are being stored up for you, ready to be released when you least expect them!

Life Application

1. What opposition are you dealing with? Pray and put it/them in God's hands.
2. Do you find yourself admiring any wrongdoers? If so, repent, pray and ask God to help you to not admire wrongdoing. Ask God to help you to desire and admire what is good in His sight.

Bonita M. Sparks Adams

Journal Reflection

After reading and/or following this devotional, write what you have learned and/or experienced.

_____
_____
_____
_____
_____
_____
_____
_____
_____
_____
_____
_____
_____
_____
_____
_____
_____

(Read Psalm 37:2)
Lesson 2:
Difficult People

Not willing to cooperate, challenging you, stubborn, rebellious, disrespectful, undermining, negative or bad attitude. The list could go on. You've been around these people, and some of them are right in your family or household!

Difficult people can make your life miserable—if you let them. When we encounter difficult people, remember that you cannot make them change. You can, however, change how you allow them to affect you! Green plants only stay that way if they are thriving in the right environment – proper soil, sunlight and water! If you remove any one of these things, that green plant is prone to wither. If withheld long enough, it will die!

Overwhelmed?

Pray for that difficult person. Many times, there are things going on with them that cause them to act as they do. It can be a misunderstanding. As you pray for them, God will start working on you and He will work on them. He may soften your heart or reveal something to you about them. He may do the same thing for them. The more you pray, eventually, their actions won't affect you the same way. That thing causing that difficult attribute to thrive will be removed. You may also feel different about them and even see changes take place in them. It will be as though their difficult behavior died or withered away!

Life Application

1. Think of a difficult person(s). List their name(s) and make a commitment to pray for them every day for one week (or longer, if you like).
2. Journal what comes to you about this person. Make a note of any changes in behavior or attitude, in yourself or in them.

Bonita M. Sparks Adams

Journal Reflection

After reading and/or following this devotional, write what you have learned and/or experienced.

_____
_____
_____
_____
_____
_____
_____
_____
_____
_____
_____
_____
_____
_____
_____
_____
_____

(Read Psalm 37:3)
Lesson 3:
Feeling Insecure

Not confident, uncertain, unsafe, shaky, threatened, overcome by fear and/or anxiety.

I am sure you would agree with Webster that these words define how you feel when you are *feeling insecure*. Trusting in the Lord allows you to experience the complete opposite—confident, certain, safe, stable, secure, unafraid, unconcerned. But, how? By recognizing that whatever is making you feel insecure, the Lord is not only able to take care of it—but he is also willing to take care of it for you.

We are like sheep, and the Lord is our shepherd. Sheep are very insecure and never feel safe. They have good reason. They have no natural abilities to fight off predators! A good shepherd keeps

Overwhelmed?

them safe from predators. That is exactly what the Lord will do for us if we let Him. In addition, a good shepherd leads the sheep to enjoy safe pastures. A good shepherd keeps sheep safe from all manner of physical harm and from eating the wrong things.

Sheep need to graze or eat constantly. They would eat anything if it were not for the shepherd. We, too, sometimes digest things (food, things we see, things we read, activities we partake in, etc.) that are harmful to us; therefore, we need the Lord to help steer us away from these things. Without a shepherd, they would just stay in one place, eating. When they have eaten everything in that pasture, they might come close to starving because they wouldn't know where to go for more food without the guidance of a shepherd. We need to trust Him with our lives and allow Him to lead us. He desires to take us to green, safe pastures!

Life Application

1. What things are causing you to feel insecure right now?
2. Confess the following, until you see the reality of it in your life.

Bonita M. Sparks Adams

"Lord, I give to you (list what or who has made you feel insecure):

_____

_____

_____

_____

_____

I no longer feel insecure about these things because I trust that you love me. Because you are with me, I don't have to be afraid. You are bigger and more powerful than anything that I am facing. You are willing and able to provide what I need to get through this. Your desire is for me to dwell in a safe place, so I allow you to lead me to that place. Thank you for peace. I trust you and surrender all to you."

Bonita M. Sparks Adams

Journal Reflection

After reading and/or following this devotional, write what you have learned and/or experienced.

_____
_____
_____
_____
_____
_____
_____
_____
_____
_____
_____
_____
_____
_____
_____
_____
_____

(Read Psalm 37:4)
Lesson 4:
What About What I Want?

Sometimes, you can do so much for others that it seems like your wants and needs get lost in the process. Sometimes, you have to learn to say, "No," for the sake of your own health, sanity and well-being. However, you have to be careful to not go overboard with focusing on yourself. The Lord wants us to do things for others. We have to change our mindset to the fact that, when we are doing for others, we are doing it for the Lord (Colossians 3:23). Seek His direction on what we should do, when we should do it, and for whom. We might be surprised to find that He doesn't want us doing all the things we are doing!

Overwhelmed?

What we do is not going unnoticed by the Lord! I love my husband and my children. They bring joy, pleasure and satisfaction to my life. Therefore, I want to do things for them that make them happy! The same is true for the Lord. When we truly find joy, pleasure and satisfaction from serving and including Him in all aspects of our lives, He will give us what makes us happy—the desires of our heart! Unfortunately, sometimes we are selfish and only care about what we want or need. Also, we can be guilty of looking to other things outside of the Lord to bring us fulfillment. It's not that we can't find happiness in other things. The problem comes when those things are more important than cultivating a relationship with the Lord. It becomes a problem when other things we're doing for our own pleasure are in direct conflict with God's will for our lives.

Another way of looking at this is that, when our relationship with the Lord is very close, He will put desires in our heart. We will begin to desire the things *He* desires. My husband and I married young. We have spent so much time together that we now desire some of the same things. What he wants, I want, and vice versa. It doesn't take away our individuality; but, in some things, we have become one. This can happen with the Lord. As you become one with Him, you will find yourself finding joy, pleasure and happiness in desiring the same things He desires.

Life Application

1. Make a list of a few things you believe the Lord did for you that made you happy.

_____
_____
_____
_____
_____
_____
_____
_____
_____

2. Just like He did these things for you, He wants to do more things for you because He loves you. However, you have to allow Him space in your life. He wants you to include Him in every aspect of your life, just like you would do for a friend, spouse, child or a close family member.

Overwhelmed?

Name one thing you would be willing to commit to doing that you believe would bring delight to the Lord. Feel free to commit to more than one thing.

_____
_____
_____
_____
_____
_____
_____
_____
_____
_____

Bonita M. Sparks Adams

Journal Reflection

After reading and/or following this devotional, write what you have learned and/or experienced.

_____
_____
_____
_____
_____
_____
_____
_____
_____
_____
_____
_____
_____
_____
_____
_____

(Read Psalm 37:5-6)
Lesson 5:
Deadline Approaching

Bills due. Evaluation. Event planning. Work to be done. Results revealed. Assignment completed. Taxes filed. Making a final decision. Any one of these can make one feel overwhelmed if we don't believe we will meet the deadline. Sometimes, our inability to meet the deadline is our own fault. Sometimes, we had no control over things that occurred that caused us to be where we are. We are faced with situations daily, and we must choose wisely in how we are going to handle these situations. Sometimes, we may not have the means (finances, ability, knowledge, etc.) or we don't know the right way. We may take shortcuts or look for easy routes that ultimately take us in the wrong direction. We may procrastinate and no longer have adequate time.

Overwhelmed?

We must learn how to seek the Lord in the way we should handle things and trust Him. Just like we would solve a problem for someone we love if we were able, or advise them on the right way to handle a matter, the Lord will do the same thing for us, if we allow Him.

Life Application

1. What are you facing right now that has a deadline?

   _____

   _____

   _____

   _____

   _____

2. Pray and ask God how you should handle it. Write here what you believe He tells you or reveals to you.

   _____

   _____

   _____

   _____

   _____

Bonita M. Sparks Adams

Journal Reflection

After reading and/or following this devotional, write what you have learned and/or experienced.

(Read Psalm 37:7)
Lesson 6:
Financial Problems

"*It's not fair! How is it that I try to do what's right, and I'm struggling to make ends meet, and Jane Doe is living raggedy and/or breaking the law, and she's living good? I work every day and can't afford designer clothing and other luxuries. But Jane Doe, who is not working, is carrying that designer purse and wearing those name brand shoes?*"

Years ago when I made less money, I thought that if only I made XYZ dollars, all my problems would be solved. When I made XYZ amount of money, I still didn't have enough money. When my children were young, at birthdays and Christmastime, I would try to make those days special and give them the best gifts I could afford.

Overwhelmed?

I did this because I loved them and I wanted to see them happy. In the same way, God loves us and wants us to be happy. Therefore, God wants to give us good gifts and make sure all of our needs are met. God owns everything in this world. We must learn to be still (which means to stop moving), get quiet, be calm and wait patiently for the Lord. He is willing and able to help us with our financial problems! We can't worry about those who are doing wrong and prospering from it. It's only for a season, and they will have to answer to God for it.

Life Application

1. Read Philippians 4:19 and write the verse here. Memorize it. Believe it.

_____
_____
_____
_____
_____
_____
_____
_____
_____

2. Give your financial concerns to God in prayer and list them here. Every time that concern comes up or crosses your mind, quote Philippians 4:19.

_____
_____
_____
_____
_____
_____
_____
_____
_____

Bonita M. Sparks Adams

Journal Reflection

After reading and/or following this devotional, write what you have learned and/or experienced.

_____
_____
_____
_____
_____
_____
_____
_____
_____
_____
_____
_____
_____
_____
_____
_____

(Read Psalm 37:8)

Lesson 7:
Angry & Stressed Out

"*What is happening to me? I find myself going from 0 to 10 in seconds, getting mad about something and getting ready to fight when I used to be so easy going!*"

That was me. I later discovered that hormonal changes, due to aging, could have been the reason. According to Better Health Channel (betterhealth.vic.gov.au), "Anger triggers the body's 'fight or flight' response. The adrenal glands flood the body with stress hormones, such as adrenaline and cortisol. The brain directs blood to the muscles in preparation for physical exertion, which could lead to attacking someone. Heart rate, blood pressure, respiration and body temperature all rise. Over time, this causes harm to your body.

Overwhelmed?

These are some of the problems that can come with unmanaged anger:

- Headaches
- Depression
- Digestion Problems
- High Blood Pressure
- Insomnia
- Skin Problems (Ex. Eczema)
- Increased Anxiety
- Stroke
- Heart Attack

Health challenges can result from injuries, disease, exposure to harmful substances and more. However, many health challenges are caused from stress! Stress can lead to anger. We have to learn how to manage and control our anger. Uncontrolled anger not only can lead to us harming others, but we can also cause our own bodies to be harmed from its effects.

When you're feeling angry, try doing the following:
1) **Stop** before responding.
2) **Ask** God, "Take away my anger and put my mind on you."

3) **Say**, "I choose *peace*! Keep my mind in perfect peace! I trust you!" (Repeat as needed)

Life Application

1) What or who triggers anger in you? List them below. Next to each item, write why you think these things anger you.

_____
_____
_____
_____
_____

2) Pray and ask God to help you in each of these areas. Ask God to reveal to you the root of why these things anger you and what you need to do. Be willing to do what He tells you.

_____
_____
_____
_____
_____

Bonita M. Sparks Adams

Journal Reflection

After reading and/or following this devotional, write what you have learned and/or experienced.

(Read Psalm 37:9-11)
Lesson 8:
Not Enough...
I Need More

Not enough money. Not enough help. Not enough time. Not enough energy. Not enough protection. Not enough food.

Lacking the things you need can cause you to not be at peace. Being in lack makes you feel insecure or unsafe. You may experience fear and feel overwhelmed! When you don't have enough, you tend to look at others and what they have. You may feel that the ones who do have should help you. Although this is true, to an extent, because God wants us to help those in need when we're able, we must be careful not to *make* others responsible for what we need. This could lead to

Overwhelmed?

resentment when others don't readily come to our aid. Sometimes, people don't have as much as we think!

We must look to the Lord to meet our every need. Let God move upon the hearts of those He chooses to meet our need. Don't limit God! He might want to provide for you in some miraculous way! Sometimes, we may look at those who aren't living right, according to our standards, and it looks like they have more than enough. This could evoke that "life isn't fair" or "God isn't fair" type of feeling. You may be tempted to do wrong to get more.

When we don't have enough, maybe God allowed it because He wants to show how willing and able He is to provide for us if we will put our hope and trust in Him. These verses remind us that the wicked only prosper for a while. It's temporary, like someone allowing you to use something of theirs. Those who are meek—those who endure with patience and put their hope in the Lord—are promised to inherit the land. An inheritance gives you ownership of something. Not only is it a permanent situation; it is a better situation.

Life Application

1. In what areas are you feeling overwhelmed due to lack?

   _____
   _____
   _____
   _____
   _____

2. Read the following Scriptures for encouragement. What does each Scripture promise?

   Philippians 4:19:

   _____
   _____
   _____

   Matthew 7:7:

   _____
   _____
   _____

   Psalm 46:1:

   _____
   _____
   _____

Bonita M. Sparks Adams

Journal Reflection

After reading and/or following this devotional, write what you have learned and/or experienced.

_____
_____
_____
_____
_____
_____
_____
_____
_____
_____
_____
_____
_____
_____
_____
_____

(Read Psalm 37:12-15)

Lesson 9:
Plotting & Scheming Against Me

My four-year old granddaughter, Aria, is such a delight. She is very bright. On one occasion, she told us that she knows *everything*! I guess she is following in her mother's footsteps, too. Imagine her, or any four-year old for that matter, threatening a six-foot, 250-pound man about what they are going to do to them. You would probably laugh. This is what God does when others are plotting and scheming against us when we are trying to live uprightly.

Although we may be aware of people plotting and scheming against us, sometimes we are not even aware that it is taking place behind closed doors or on the phone. God sees everything! No matter how discreet and secretive others may think they are, God not only sees it, but He hears it and He knows the thoughts of man. Don't worry about what others are trying to do to you. Let God handle it. When we take matters into our own hands, we make a mess of things. Sometimes, we look like the bad guy. Be encouraged because God promises in this Psalm that when others, "draw their swords or bend their bows to cast us down, their swords are going to end up in their own hearts and their bows will be broken" (Isaiah 54:17). This lets us know that, "Weapons may be formed against us, but they won't be successful in their intent. In addition, every tongue that speaks against you in judgment, you will condemn!"

Life Application

1. Do you know of or suspect people plotting against you? Pray now and place them and that situation in God's hands.

---

2. Encourage yourself by reading Psalm 37:12-15, Psalm 110:1 and Isaiah 54:17. What encouragement do you get from these Scriptures?

_____

_____

_____

_____

_____

Bonita M. Sparks Adams

Journal Reflection

After reading and/or following this devotional, write what you have learned and/or experienced.

(Read Psalm 37:16)

Lesson 10: Stuck & Not Moving Forward

Have you ever thought to yourself, "I thought by now I would be further ahead in my life than this"? Perhaps your life has not advanced to the degree you had envisioned and you appear to be stuck. Sometimes, we are where we are because we are dealing with consequences of bad choices. Sometimes, we have not taken the right steps to prepare ourselves to move forward. There were times when we allowed fear to hold us back. However, sometimes, we are right where God wants us to be!

We have a tendency to compare ourselves to others. When we do that, we don't recognize

Overwhelmed?

our blessings because what we have looks small compared to what others may have. However, there is always someone less fortunate than us, and they are looking at you, wishing they had what you have! It appears that we are not moving forward because we may not recognize that God is using what is happening right now to mold, shape and train us for where He is taking us. Some people have what they have or are in certain positions due to unlawful or dishonest practices. This Psalm reminds us that, "It is better to have a little and be doing what is right in God's eyes than to have the riches of those who are not living right."

Life Application

1. Name the area(s) where you feel you have absolutely no forward movement. Where do you feel stuck? Pray and ask God to reveal to you why this is the case.

   _____
   _____
   _____
   _____
   _____

2. Meditate on these Scriptures. What does God reveal to you?

   Philippians 4:11:

   _____
   _____
   _____
   _____
   _____

   Hebrews 13:5:

   _____
   _____
   _____
   _____

   Romans 8:28:

   _____
   _____
   _____
   _____

   Ephesians 1:11:

   _____
   _____
   _____
   _____

Bonita M. Sparks Adams

Journal Reflection

After reading and/or following this devotional, write what you have learned and/or experienced.

(Read Psalm 37:17)
Lesson 11:
I'm So Tired of This

Are you listening, God? Do you see what I'm going through? Nothing is changing. I can't take anymore. I'm so tired of this!

This is how you sometimes feel when you have been dealing with an unpleasant person or situation for a long time. Sometimes, the more you pray or try to do right, the worse the situation seems to get. This is a deception from the enemy (the devil) to get you to stop doing what you are doing because it is working for your good!

In Mark 9:20-26, they brought a boy to Jesus who had an evil spirit. *When the spirit saw Jesus, it threw the boy into a convulsion, caused him to fall to the ground and roll around foaming at the*

Overwhelmed?

mouth. The situation appeared worse before it got better, but the spirit did leave because Jesus commanded it to do so!

This psalm reminds us that the power of the wicked will be broken! It does not matter what it looks like to you! There is still power in the name of Jesus! When we call on the name of Jesus, evil spirits have to go! You feel tired because it hasn't changed quickly enough for you. However, many times, changes are taking place in the spirit realm or internally that you can't see right away. This psalm reminds us that the Lord is holding up the righteous. You and your situation are in His capable hands! Quit trying to do the work yourself; trust and allow Him to work it out!

Life Application

1. Reflect on a situation(s) that you're tired of dealing with. Write about it here.

_____
_____
_____
_____
_____

2. Imagine God's hands as two big hands. One hand has you in it; He is holding you and nothing can happen to you without Him allowing it. He's got it and will work it out for you. Pray these points:
   - Put the situation(s) in the Lord's hands.
   - Ask the Lord to help you to leave it with Him and to totally trust Him to work it out.
   - Ask the Lord to reveal what He wants you to do or not to do moving forward.
   - Ask the Lord to remove all negative feelings, doubt, unbelief and hurt you're harboring against someone.
   - Ask the Lord to give you new eyes to see the situation in a new light so you can see what He is doing versus what you want it to be.
   - Ask the Lord to guard your heart and mind.
   - Thank the Lord for what you believe He is doing. Make positive confessions as though everything you want is already done.

Bonita M. Sparks Adams

Journal Reflection

After reading and/or following this devotional, write what you have learned and/or experienced.

PART 2:
GOD'S PROMISES TO ME

(Read Psalm 37:18)

Lesson 12:
God's Promise to Me: "I'm Under His Care"

When someone is under the care of another person or entity, they are responsible for providing the needs, wants and desires of that individual. Sometimes, this responsibility is because they are the parent or legal guardian, or because of their occupation. For example, a doctor, nurse or teacher is required to meet the needs of those they serve. Some of their responsibilities are bound by law! This psalm reminds us that we are under the Lord's care—not only today, but forever.

Reflect on the following situations. Pray and write what God reveals to you.

Overwhelmed?

1. Children are under the care of their parents. What does this mean? How long does this responsibility last?

   _____
   _____
   _____
   _____
   _____

2. Sometimes, people are under the care of the state or government (i.e., foster children, government employees, military, inmates, parolees, etc.). What does this mean? How long does this responsibility last?

   _____
   _____
   _____
   _____
   _____

3. God is our Father. What does this mean? How long does this responsibility last?

   _____
   _____
   _____
   _____
   _____

4. How can these situations relate to how God cares for us?

5. This psalm says we have an eternal inheritance. What's good about having an inheritance?

6. What have you gained from this?

(Read Psalm 37:19)
Lesson 13:
God's Promise to Me: "I Have Plenty"

According to Merriam-Webster Dictionary, a disaster is defined as a "sudden event bringing great damage, loss, or destruction; misfortune or failure." We may experience disasters that happen without warning. This psalm reminds us that when these events take place, God promises that we will not wither and die from it.

I am not the best person to keep plants alive. I forget to water them. However, I am amazed at times when I water a plant that's on the verge of dying. It seems to come back to life! The Word of God is likened to water. The Word freshens and gives life, just like water does. If I believe the

Overwhelmed?

Word of God, and apply it to situations I am going through, I will be renewed and restored. I will not die from my situations!

In addition, this psalm reminds us that God promises us plenty! When I hear the word "plenty," I think of more than enough, as opposed to a "famine," which means there is a shortage. God owns this world and everything in it. If you need something, He will provide it. For example, let's say I have hundreds of pencils. If my child doesn't have a pencil and needs one, I will give them one or two pencils. As long as I have them, you might as well say they also have plenty because I will provide for them each time they ask. Just like a parent, God promises to meet our every need.

Reflect on the following situations. Pray and write what God reveals to you.

1. If you had an abundance of something, and your child needed it, what would you do?

   _____
   _____
   _____
   _____
   _____

2. Think about an area of your life where you don't have enough of something you need. Write it here.

___

3. Imagine God having an abundance of that item you're lacking, along with His unconditional love for you. Why should this bring peace and comfort to you?

___

(Read Psalm 37:20)

Lesson 14: God's Promise to Me: "My Enemies Will Be Dealt With"

When people hurt you, especially multiple times, a part of you may want revenge or to avoid them altogether. Don't seek revenge. God said, "Vengeance is mine. I will repay them" (Romans 12:19). We make matters worse when we try to get back at people. Sometimes, we end up looking like the bad one or suffering consequences from our bad actions.

On several occasions, God has taken care of people who wronged me. What He did took care of them and the situation in ways I would have

Overwhelmed?

never thought of! People can make your life miserable if you let them! Don't let them. You can't change people, but you can change how you react to what they do to you. Many times, the enemy (the devil) is using them to get at you. He is using them to upset you, discourage you and distract you from doing what God wants you to do. That's why we are encouraged to, "Pray for our enemies and those who despitefully use us" (Matthew 5:44).

Doing this brings God into the picture to work on our behalf. It also changes us and how we feel about them.

This psalm reminds us that our enemies are temporary, just like flowers are here one day and later, they wither and die. Flowers die when their season is over or if they lose the proper sunlight, water or temperature. Just like how God controls the things needed for flowers to live, God controls how long our enemies are able to do what they do. He will take care of them; their days are numbered!

Reflect on the following situations. Pray and write what God reveals to you.

Bonita M. Sparks Adams

1. Who would you consider as your enemies?

   _____
   _____
   _____
   _____
   _____

2. How have you been dealing with your enemies?

   _____
   _____
   _____
   _____
   _____

3. After this lesson, what will you do about your enemies?

   _____
   _____
   _____
   _____
   _____

(Read Psalm 37:21-22)

Lesson 15:
God's Promise to Me: "I Have an Inheritance"

Can I borrow $50 until I get paid on Friday? Friday comes, and they don't repay you. This can make you feel "some kind of way," especially if it has happened more than once.

If I am honest, there were times when I borrowed money and really planned to pay it back, but couldn't. I found that it's best to let that person know you're unable to pay it back. Tell them when you can repay it, or just be honest when you originally ask and say you won't be able to pay it back. This psalm calls people "wicked" who borrow and don't repay it...*yikes...ouch!* The righteous are defined as those who give generously. This psalm

Overwhelmed?

also states that, "The Lord blesses them to inherit the land."

Several Scriptures talk about the righteous having an inheritance. Knowing you have an inheritance gives you a sense of security and something to look forward to. The people I know who were the benefactors of an inheritance were placed in a better position than they were before. They were able to do some things they had dreamed about doing. An inheritance can make dreams come true. The inheritance the righteous will receive is for the present and future. The legacy that Jesus provided for us by dying on the cross for our sins brought us forgiveness, the ability to be in right relationship with God, and the curse of poverty and sickness is broken off of us.

An exchange took place. Jesus' body was broken so our bodies could be healed. He died so we could live. The future legacy that was provided came from His resurrection. Jesus conquered death and made it possible for every believer to now have eternal life. Death and the grave would not hold them! Since, "Jesus was obedient to death on the cross, His name became highly exalted. Anything we ask in Jesus' name will be done." All the promises believers receive through Jesus help dreams to come true, bring security, and provide something to look forward to both now and in the future.

Reflect on the following situations. Pray and write what God reveals to you.

1. How would things change for you if you found out you had an inheritance of one million dollars?

   _____
   _____
   _____
   _____
   _____

2. An inheritance is usually left for close relatives and/or friends. A spiritual inheritance is for believers who have a personal relationship with the Lord. Have you ever asked to be forgiven for all your sins and invited Jesus into your heart to be your Lord and Savior? Meditate on the following Scriptures. Write what you believe the Scripture is saying to you and/or what you need to do.

Overwhelmed?

John 3:16

_____
_____
_____
_____

Romans 6:23

_____
_____
_____
_____

Romans 10:9-10

_____
_____
_____
_____

1 John 1:9

_____
_____
_____
_____

Bonita M. Sparks Adams

Revelation 3:20

_____
_____
_____
_____
_____

(Read Psalm 37:23-24)
Lesson 16:
God's Promise to Me: "He's Holding Me Up"

Today is Friday, February 1, 2019. For the last four days, schools have been closed due to inclement weather. For the last two days, our city was shut down, with several businesses and city offices closed due to extremely cold, below-zero temperatures. I went outside to get something out of my car and there was a sheet of ice on the ground. I carefully took each step, in fear of falling. I slid a couple of times, but was able to keep my balance and did not fall. I wish this was the case a week ago when, in an auditorium where I was the speaker, I tripped on a cord, stumbled

Overwhelmed?

and fell in front of a group of teenage girls. Talk about an embarrassing moment; this was definitely one of those moments. However, I turned it into a teachable moment by telling them that, in life, you may stumble and fall, but you have to get up and keep it moving.

However, this psalm encourages us by saying something different. This psalm tells us that the Lord is holding our hand. He makes our steps steady and, although we may stumble, we will not fall. This promise is for those who "delight" in the Lord. In other words, the Lord is holding the hand of those who find pleasure, enjoyment, happiness and contentment in Him. If we delight in the Lord, we will want to spend time with Him. We will read and study His Word (the Bible). Just like I was slipping on the ice and did not fall, applying God's Word and His principles of living will keep you standing when you encounter slippery situations, stumbling blocks and pitfalls.

Reflect on the following situations. Pray and write what God reveals to you.

1. What situations are you dealing with right now that you need God to hold you up for fear of falling?

   _____
   _____
   _____
   _____
   _____

2. Imagine God having a big hand. You are in the middle of His hand and He's holding you. How does this bring comfort to you?

   _____
   _____
   _____
   _____
   _____

(Read Psalm 37:25-26)

Lesson 17:
God's Promise to Me: "He Will Not Forsake Me"

After reflecting over my life, God has never forsaken me or those close to me. Forsake means to "turn away from; abandon; leave." I will admit that there are times when God appears to be silent and doesn't answer right away, or he doesn't move in the way I would like. Even in those times, I've realized that He was always right there with me, working things out in a way that would be best for me. We can't see the end from the beginning like God can; yet, we try to dictate to God how things should play out in our lives.

Overwhelmed?

One time, I was praying for a new job. Time was passing and nothing was happening. Nothing was changing. In times like this, you feel like, *"Where are you Lord?"* Finally, a wonderful job opportunity came with a big firm that paid a lot more money than I was making. This had to be it! The Lord also helped me have a great interview. I was sure I had the job. It was such a letdown when I didn't get it.

A couple of weeks later, out of the blue, another opportunity came up and I got that job. It turned out to be a much better opportunity for me. I became a school secretary. This job paid more money than my current job; it had better benefits and, the best benefit of all, I was off work when my children were off! Not to mention, I later became a teacher. The 10+ years I worked as a school secretary could be combined with my years of teaching, allowing me to retire sooner!

A couple of months later, after I didn't get the original job I wanted, I found out they had a massive layoff. I would have been laid off if I got the other job. God is always looking out for what will benefit us most. In addition, when we try to live righteously, He blesses our children as well. I have been able to share this testimony with my own children, and it has helped them in similar situations. They have had the same results when they trusted God. As God blesses us, we should bless others. He will bless us and our children even more!

Reflect on the following situations. Pray and write what God reveals to you.

1. Is there an area you feel God has been silent on in your life or an area where He hasn't answered your prayer yet? Explain here.

_____
_____
_____
_____
_____

2. After reading this lesson and meditating on the following verses, write what you now believe.

    Romans 8:28:

_____
_____
_____
_____
_____

Overwhelmed?

2 Corinthians 9:8:

Philippians 4:19:

Deuteronomy 15:10:

(Read Psalm 37:27 & 29)

Lesson 18:
God's Promise to Me: "He Has a Place for Me"

My heart goes out to the homeless.

As a community service project, one day, we stayed outside all day to bring awareness to homelessness and collected money for a homeless shelter. It was rainy and cold, and we were uncomfortable; however, when the day was over, we each had a home to go to. There is a level of comfort that a home provides that you take for granted until it is not there. When I look back over my life, there were occasions where we had to leave our home and stay with relatives temporarily. Even if their homes were "better" than our home, we were happy when we could go back

Overwhelmed?

to our own home. As the saying goes, "There is no place like home."

When this psalm was written, people didn't always feel secure about where they were living. There was always the possibility of another nation or someone stronger coming along to either force you off the land, kill you for the land, fight you for the land, and/or take the land and enslave you. This psalm promises that, if you turn from evil and do good, the Lord will allow you to dwell in the land forever. The Lord will provide a place for us to dwell in this life and the one to come after we die. You can experience peace and feel secure if you believe this.

In John 14:2-3, Jesus tells us that, "There are many mansions in God's house and He has gone to prepare a place for us. One day, He will come back for us so that where He is we will be also."

Reflect on the following situations. Pray and write what God reveals to you.

1. Think of a time when you felt either "out of place" or literally had "no place to live." Explain how this made you feel.

   _____
   _____
   _____
   _____
   _____

2. Meditate on the fact that God has a place for you now and for all eternity. Explain how this makes you feel.

   _____
   _____
   _____
   _____
   _____

(Read Psalm 37:28)
Lesson 19:
God's Promise to Me: "He Loves Me"

Betty is diagnosed with a disease. She is in and out of the hospital and needs a lot of care. Her husband, David, can't take the stress of it, so he leaves her. Derrick is out of work and can't find a good paying job. The stress of the bad financial situation causes his wife, Mary, to leave him. It's easy to be with someone when things are going good, but what about when times are bad? Bad can mean the things listed above or that the person is unpleasant to be around. Some situations are very hard to endure. But, when you love someone, you try not to abandon them. This psalm reassures us that the Lord will never abandon or forsake us. Another Scripture tells us that

Overwhelmed?

nothing can separate us from the love of God. How comforting it is to know that, no matter how bad we mess up, the Lord loves us and will not leave us.

This psalm also tells us that God loves justice. He will work on the behalf of those who are in the right. When faced with an injustice, we must trust Him to handle it. Romans 12:19 says, "Vengeance is mine. I will repay, says the Lord." When we take matters into our own hands, we can make the situation worse and, ultimately, suffer the consequences of our actions.

Finally, this psalm tells us that, not only will the wicked be cut off, but their descendants will be cut off, as well. However, when we are in right relationship with God, we are not only blessed, but our descendants will be blessed, too!

Reflect on the following situations. Pray and write what God reveals to you.

1. "If we who are earthy know how to do good things for those we love, how much more would our Heavenly Father do for us?" (Matthew 7:11)
    a. Think about someone you love. If they were in trouble or needed your help, write

below to what extent you would go to help them out.

_____
_____
_____

b. Think of a situation you are dealing with right now. What comfort does it provide to know that God loves you, will not abandon or forsake you, and has unlimited power and resources to meet your every need?

_____
_____
_____

2. Since blessings and cursings can be passed down through generations, how will knowing this influence your behavior?

_____
_____
_____
_____

(Read Psalm 37:30)
Lesson 20:
God's Promise to Me: "I Am Wise"

People can say some stupid stuff! Have you ever sat and observed people and their conversations? Try it sometimes. You would be amazed and amused! Do you know someone who is intelligent, but lacks common sense? If given the choice between intelligence and wisdom, I believe wisdom is far better. You can know stuff, but you need to know how to *apply* that knowledge in the right way in the right situations. The Bible says in James 1:5 that, "If we lack wisdom, all we have to do is ask for it and God will give it to us liberally." When I went back to school to finish my bachelor's degree, if I didn't understand something, I would ask

Overwhelmed?

God to give me wisdom and understanding in the matter, and He would do it! I graduated with honors!

God is "omniscient," which means that He is all-knowing. Since He is all-knowing, we should seek His direction in all matters. We can avoid many pitfalls and make wise decisions if we allow Him to direct our paths. God has helped me on countless occasions! He is also a just (lawful) God. This psalm promises us that if we are righteous (in right standing with God), we speak wisdom and talk of justice. As His ambassadors on this earth, our conversations and lifestyle should display God's wisdom and justice.

Reflect on the following situations. Pray and write what God reveals to you.

1. List some areas you need wisdom in.

_____
_____
_____
_____
_____

2. Pray and ask God for the wisdom needed for each area listed above. As He gives it to you or reveals what you should do, date and record it here.

_____
_____
_____
_____
_____

(Read Psalm 37:31)

Lesson 21:
God's Promise to Me: "He is in My Heart So I Walk Right"

I hate when it is icy outside! This past winter, I went to someone's home for the first time to pick up something. I've never seen a steeper driveway leading up to a front door at the top of a hill. Although they had put salt down, it barely melted the ice. It was very scary walking up the driveway. Although I was in a hurry, I had to calculate each step and walk ever so carefully. I went back and forth between the grass, steps and driveway to avoid slippery spots as I made my way to the top. Victory came! I made it to the top without falling—only to find out I was at the wrong house.

Overwhelmed?

Going down was even worse! I had to make a similar trek again up the hill to the front door of the right house, which was next door! However, at least that house had a railing to hold on to once I got halfway up the hill.

When God's Word or law is in our heart, and we live according to what it says, it will stabilize us. It will make our steps sure and keep us from sliding and falling! Situations may arise and cause us to feel unsteady and unsure of what to do. We may even experience fear. God's word has an answer for everything we will ever face! If we apply it to our lives, it will provide peace and stability for us. When we have a personal relationship with Jesus, and He is residing in our heart, we will not only walk right, but our steps will be sure and steady. When the storms of life blow, we will be planted like a tree and not be moved!

Reflect on the following situations. Pray and write what God reveals to you.

1. Every Bible usually has a concordance in the back for looking up Scriptures based on key words. Use the concordance or search Google for Scriptures pertaining to your current situation. Write the scriptures below.

Bonita M. Sparks Adams

2. Meditate on these Scriptures all week. If possible, commit them to memory. Write below the results of doing this.

(Read Psalm 37:32-33)

Lesson 22:
God's Promise to Me: "Wicked Will Not Triumph Over Me"

I watched a video on how lions hunt their prey. Lions usually attack at night. They stalk and watch their prey, and usually they attack only when they are within a certain proximity. They like striking when an animal is alone. Lions often work in pairs or in groups when going for larger prey.

The Scripture says our enemy, the devil, walks around like a roaring lion, seeking whom he may devour. The devil watches us, stalks us and tries to separate us from others we draw strength from. He likes to strike against us at night, in the dark or in a hidden way. He tries to rally others to join

Overwhelmed?

forces against us—others being actual people or thoughts that bombard our mind. The good news is that we are never alone. God is always watching and has our back.

This psalm says that, even when the wicked are going out of their way to slay us or do us harm, the Lord will not leave us in their hand. In addition, Isaiah 54:17 promises us that, "Even though the enemy may form weapons against us, they will not prosper against us and every tongue that rises against us in judgment, we will condemn. This is our heritage (legacy or inheritance) as servants of the Lord." Psalm 23:5 tells us that the Lord will, "Prepare a table for us in the presence of our enemies." In other words, He will bless us and work on our behalf right in front of our enemies!

Reflect on the following situations. Pray and write what God reveals to you.

1. List people or situations working against you.

_____
_____
_____
_____
_____

2. Meditate and commit to memory these Scriptures. What is God saying to you?

   Psalm 37:32-33

   Isaiah 54:17

   Psalm 23:5

(Read Psalm 37:34)

Lesson 23:
God's Promise to Me: "He Will Exalt Me"

Whatever you want to happen in your life, sometimes it's hard to wait for it, especially if you have been waiting on it for a long time. I know firsthand what it's like to work hard, make great sacrifices, gladly help others and do all I know to do, and still can't seem to get a break! After many years in the game, I felt like I was moving backward.

You, too, may have experienced this. You see others making moves and advancing. Even those who are not even as good as you—so you think. Strangers may have even prophesied over you and told you these things were going to come to pass; but years are passing by, you are getting older, and

Overwhelmed?

it doesn't seem like the right doors are opening. Don't get discouraged! Wait on the Lord! He will bring it to pass when the time is right!

Everything that is happening in your life is exactly the way it is supposed to be. Where you are right now is the best place for you. We have a tendency to feel like, when we get to this exalted place, then we will be successful. The truth is if you are allowing God to use you, each step of this process is important as He is grooming, preparing and positioning you. Everyone you come in contact with at each step is important. If we get impatient and try to make things happen before His appointed time, we are setting ourselves up for failure. If we look to people to make things happen for us, we are indebted to them. They may turn on us or not have our best interests at heart. The world can be cut throat and make you feel like you have to step on others or only think about yourself to get ahead. We must stay humble, keep following God and His ways, and let Him exalt us. In due season, it will happen in His good timing. We will inherit what He has for us. We will see His promises fulfilled and we will see the wicked cut off.

Reflect on the following situations. Pray and write what God reveals to you.

1. Read the stories of others in the Bible who waited a long time for God's promises to come to pass in their lives.
   - Abraham: Genesis chapters 16, 17 and 21
   - Joseph: Genesis chapters 37-50
   - David: I Samuel chapters 16-31 and II Samuel chapters 1-2

2. What did you learn from their stories?

   Abraham:

   _____
   _____
   _____
   _____
   _____

   Joseph:

   _____
   _____
   _____
   _____
   _____

Overwhelmed?

David:

(Read Psalm 37:35-38)

Lesson 24:
God's Promise to Me: "He Has a Good Future For Me"

As a high-school business teacher, I spend plenty of time encouraging young people to think about and prepare for their future career. When students reach their senior year, and graduation day arrives, there is so much promise for these young people and their future. Parents and other family members, friends, teachers, principals and others are happy and proud of their accomplishments. We should strive to live upright before God and follow His commands as He, too, will be happy for us. God has planned a good future for those who are obedient.

Overwhelmed?

Although, at times, it seems like the wicked are in great power and their reach is spreading, the day is coming when they will be cut off. This psalm says the future of the upright is one of peace. Peace that is not understandable. Peace that prevails in the midst of turmoil. Peace that brings rest because God has conquered all the people and things that came against you. No one knows what the future holds, but God knows. He has assured us in this psalm that we can expect a good future when we live uprightly.

Reflect on the following situations. Pray and write what God reveals to you.

1. Evaluate your life and obedience to God's Word. How do you think God would categorize you? Upright or wicked? Please explain.

_____

_____

_____

_____

We all can improve. Pray now and ask God to forgive you for your sins. Be willing to surrender all to Him and invite Him to take control of your life. Be sure to read the last lesson.

(Read Psalm 37:39-40)
Lesson 25:
God's Promise to Me: "He Saved Me"

I told myself, "I'm not going to do it again."

I was successful for a while and then, I did it again. Romans 7:15 explains that what we want to do, we don't do; and what we don't want to do, we find ourselves doing. Because of our sin nature, no matter how good we try to be, we can't be good enough. I might not say the wrong thing, or do the wrong thing, but I might think it. And that is sin, too!

> Romans 3:23 says, "For all have sinned, and fallen short of the glory of God."

According to the Scripture, the penalty for sin is death! Because God is a just, righteous king and judge, my punishment should be death!

Overwhelmed?

Romans 6:23 says, "For the wages of sin is death."

I decided that I was going to do good deeds for others, help my community and follow the steps from someone's self-help book; however, all my efforts to do right before God just look like I'm presenting Him filthy rags.

Isaiah 64:6 says, "...our righteous acts are like filthy rags."

This psalm tells us the Lord will help us and deliver us! God loved us so much that He sent His Son, Jesus, to be our substitute and pay the penalty of our sins. If we believe in Jesus, and what He did for us, we can have everlasting life!

Romans 5:8 says, "God demonstrated his love toward us in while we were sinners, Christ died for us."

John 3:16 says, "For God so loved the world, that He gave his only begotten son, that whosoever believeth in Him, should not perish, but they should have everlasting life."

Bonita M. Sparks Adams

This psalm tells us that our salvation is in the Lord. Jesus is the only way. He will save those who trust in Him.

> John 14:6 says, "Jesus said, 'I am the way, and the truth, and the life, no one comes to the Father but by me.'"

> John 3:3 says, "Jesus replied, 'Very truly I tell you, no one can see the kingdom of God unless they are born again.'"

> Acts 16:30-31 says, "A jailer asked Paul and Silas: 'Sirs, what must I do to be saved?' They answered, 'Believe on the Lord Jesus Christ, and you will be saved.'"

> Romans 10:9 says, "If you confess with your mouth the Lord Jesus and believe in your heart that God has raised Him from the dead, you will be saved."

> Romans 10:13 says, "Whoever calls on the name of the Lord shall be saved."

Invite Jesus to come into your life as your Lord and Savior.

Overwhelmed?

Revelation 3:20 says, "Behold I stand at the door and knock. If anyone hears My voice and opens the door, I will come in to him and dine with him, and he with Me."

Pray this Prayer:

I know I am a sinner and ask that you please forgive me for all my sins. I believe that Jesus is your son and that He died for my sins. He was buried and rose again on the third day. I invite you to come into my life as my Lord and Savior. Please change my heart and mind to live according to your Word. I surrender to you. I invite your Holy Spirit into my life, to baptize me and empower me to be a witness for you. Help me to find a bible-believing church to help me grow.

Today, you were born again! Write the date: _____

About The Author

Bonita Marie (Sparks) Adams has an Honorary Doctorate in Ministry from Ramah Institute of Theology. She is a member of Walls Memorial Chapel AME Zion Church where her mother, Rev. Shirley A. Sparks, has served as the Pastor for over 28 years. Along with serving in several capacities at her church, Bonita is a high school business teacher.

Bonita is also an award-winning playwright. She has won several awards from Urban Playwrights United. Her play, "Obama Looks Back" was featured in the D.C. Black Theater Festival, and her play "My Mother Prayed for Me" has won an award at the A Taste of Theater Festival held at Indiana University.

Bonita also serves as a producer. She has written, produced and directed over ten stage plays, in addition to spearheading numerous Black History

Overwhelmed?

programs, dinner murder mystery shows, skits, puppet shows, award programs, and talent & fashion shows. Her play, "Exposed," which features her husband, James L. Adams as the devil, has been performed for over 20 years. Her company has collaborated with many others to bring stage plays, award programs, DVD screenings and film premieres to the Toledo local area and abroad.

As an entrepreneur, Bonita and James also founded JAB Transportation LLC, JAB ETM Productions, LLC (James and Bonita Exposing Truth Ministries Productions, LLC), and Write The Vision Publishing, LLC. She conducts classes and workshops, is a consultant and a speaker. She is also a Mary Kay Beauty Consultant.

Bonita has written educational curriculum in addition to authoring several books. Her books include:

- ACTIVATE: Secret Agents in Spiritual Warfare
- Overwhelmed? Finding Help in Psalm 37 Devotional & Journal
- Miracles: They Happen Every Day
- Aria's & Grandmommy's Adventures – Solving The Mystery of Fire: The Good & The Bad (This is a Children's Book for ages 3-8)

Bonita M. Sparks Adams

- Exposing the Truth About the Holidays thru Drama
- Exposed Bible Study Guide (An accompaniment to the stage play)

Bonita is the proud mother of LaTosha (Jason) and Tamika (Lukasz), and grandmother to Aria.

ACTIVATE: Secret Agents In Spiritual Warfare

By Bonita M. Sparks Adams

Merriam-Webster Dictionary defines activate as: (1) to make active or more active; (2) to set up or formally institute (as a military unit) with the necessary personnel and equipment; to put (an individual or unit) on active duty.

This book is designed to move you into *more* action when it comes to prayer and spiritual warfare. You may say, "I pray already" or "I already know about spiritual warfare." Inspired by the Holy Spirit, those who read and follow the instructions in this book prayerfully will be commissioned to serve in a greater capacity in God's Army.

Like a military unit waiting to be deployed into battle. Like a grenade that has been lying dormant until the pin has been pulled out. This book is designed to deploy you into active duty! It is designed to pull the pin out so you become explosive in prayer and spiritual warfare!

www.ingramcontent.com/pod-product-compliance
Lightning Source LLC
Chambersburg PA
CBHW071500080526
44587CB00014B/2164